FOR EXAMPLE

FOR EXAMPLE

ROSEMARY NORMAN

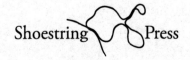
Shoestring Press

Printed by imprintdigital
Upton Pyne, Exeter
www.imprintdigital.com

Typesetting and cover design by narrator
www.narrator.me.uk
info@narrator.me.uk
033 022 300 39

Published by Shoestring Press
19 Devonshire Avenue, Beeston, Nottingham, NG9 1BS
(0115) 925 1827
www.shoestringpress.co.uk

First published 2016
© Copyright: Rosemary Norman

The moral right of the author has been asserted.

Photograph of the author by David Larcher.

ISBN 978-1-910323-59-5

ACKNOWLEDGEMENTS

Thanks to the editors of *Ambit*, *The Delinquent*, *The Interpreter's House*, *London Grip*, *The North*, *The Rialto*, *The SHOp*, *Smiths Knoll* and *South Bank Poetry*, who between them published most of the poems here, sometimes in earlier versions.

CONTENTS

ALICE'S COUCH

Alice Neel: *Andy Warhol, 1970*

After Valerie Solanas – giddy
with rightness and frank greed

for us, her sex – after her bullet
got her heard, you see Andy

took his shirt off at Alice's.
The couch lists. It's hostile, all

edges. But she'd recognised
gun-work in an altered hang of

light on cloth, evidence of flesh
sewn up askew. His cheek

she works on like a child's graze
and though it was, is unhurt

he sits still, lets her, eyes down
and mouth airily composed.

Fame nags at her. *Mistress-
piece.* Call it that, it's the same

sketchy rock, same mermaid
with two tails. She'll spare him,

if she can, the tan lace-ups
in the foreground. Eases space

that can't be, between his soles
and the lack any definite floor.

ANYHOW

Mirrors are no use
for putting on earrings.

The holes are twin
and that's enough of reflection

or I'll be over-
critical of the ear, the face,

the frame of hair, till all joy
at my dexterity

as the small healed wounds
receive their silver

is lost. I lose
earrings, of course.

Therefore
it's important to give them away

sometimes, to take charge again
of their coming and going.

Anyhow, I prefer
to have few pairs, and their design

not too various, an alteration in me
that keeps itself to itself.

AT SEA

Bas Jan Ader 1942 – 1975

No, but suppose
    he'd turned into a bird,
an albatross, human
    in its heaviness, the meat
of it, but with all
    that lift. He's no less
lost than any merely
    drowned sailor ever was
between man and bird
    and word. What he is, is
not one nor the other,
    not there, a necessary
interval to let words
    hold what sense they can
in, for breath, of course
    and for the big wings
to open and admit
    what passes for invention.

BARBER'S SHOP

It's as if
    he knows
who he is   as if a habit
of uprightness
    in the body   overrode
what the head's lost   as if
a thread ran down
    his spine   heaven
to earth   his place on it

She: let me take
    your stick
& hearing-aid &
glasses   so the young man
    here can cut
your hair   then we'll go
for cakes & coffee   Yet
    he's worn a moustache
always   against this

BIG YELLOW SELF STORAGE

Five o'clock. The man and boy
who washed it down at noon are evident

in its yellow unmediated by dirt.
Remarkable the handle on the squeegee

of the man, who cleaned
the upper part, over-long like a shadow

the high sun gave no account of.
The air is short, at odds

with gusts of wind. Trees
on the skyline show the small irregularities

of a graph as if some read-off
from the body blipped at St Matthias' spire.

THE BIRD DOOR

Nothing much to forget, oh
but the birds she'd lost

already when she wasn't
yet the one she's not now

either, with her crayons,
reminiscing as instructed –

why else? They were birds
on leaded panes, beak,

eye and wing outlined
in brown and breasts filled

with rose or amber. She'd
had to go and her birds

stayed put, their brown
bird feet gripping the twigs

drawn in for them, glass
belongs to glass. She draws

a gate but there was none.
If she recalls, wooden posts

leaned in an inch or two,
into a gap. It's not unlikely.

BLUEBEARD

It put her in mind
of loose
blue petals
as if her touch
might dislodge them

and she'd find one
curled
in her palm
like the modest
key he pressed on her

hoping, of course,
she'd go
where it led —
gowns that hang
huge up on their rail

and come to life
on him.
In this silk
hothouse, one
glove has room in it

for both her arms,
and his
high heels
set her tottering
like a child dressed up

as its own mother.
Soon
he'll be here.
His singular key
is back in their kitchen

drawer. It speaks
of love
to obscure
buttons on stubs
of cotton, safety pins.

CLOCK

He bought it for its belly
like a saucer
with face and hands

to tell the time. Also
its pendulum.
Forget what *tick-tock*

means in a cat's tail,
it looks down
equably from an upper

saucer with ears, upon
his jars
with hats for lids,

their cheeks as puffed out
as the winds',
and on his ashtrays –

Smoke Like Helen B. Merry –
seaside china
in an afterlife that's forever

kept faith with cigarettes.
She's an example
to us all, Helen B. Could

so many dainty corkscrews
be mistaken?
Not while the pink cat

presides and chimes
with its tinny
bong, on the hour,

and the old, sweet chill
at the sea's edge
still has him by the ankles.

COLLAGE

Mary Herbert: *I'd like to travel somewhere*
no-one else has ever been

As the paper yellows so do the stars.
The original blue
of the printed sky they stand in
is greener than it was
but the stars' compromised endurance

is all there is
of portal for our travellers in time,
two men in suits, city jackets
loose in an apparent heat or haste.
Sun shines grey
on what they have with them
of pond, clipped hedge
and garden nude,
its upper body left elsewhere
by a once-photographer who's now

unthinkable. No place
for any third under such stars
or under the valiant if discoloured sky
that brought the stars forth,
pressed down onto a page formerly blank.

COLLYER SYNDROME

For years now I've pretended to be good-looking
and let them make what they can of it, me as

photos of me, skipping through colour supplements
this week, next week, scrupulous as to where and

when I unfold and, often as not, making my entrance
on the arm of a detractor. I gather captions to me,

theirs among many. Between the lies, read
how they seek me out like an ill-chosen beloved.

Let them keep me on shelves, on floors, in narrowing
passageways where rooms once were. I will nest

and yellow with them and when at last they crawl
into that no-space where the ribs cannot open or shut

and the poor heart stops, let it be me that's found
there, thousands deep and not yellow but golden.

COUNTING TO A THOUSAND

If I've told you once I've told you a thousand times
she says, she says, she says, whatever it is
she's told me.

Please do this, don't do that, don't do anything, don't
not do anything, don't just stand there
doing nothing.

Oh, get out of the way she says but doesn't tell me
what the way is that I'm in. Because I would
try, I would.

Haven't you got anything to say for yourself she says
and it isn't a question, she isn't looking for
yes or no

let alone to hear me count ten for her, over and over,
not to say something we'd regret and so on, up
to a thousand.

FINE DARK STRIPE

John Torrington 1825 – 1846

If I were young
    and a man and
        square shouldered

enough I'd choose
    a shirt like his –
        the ice in its fine

stripe on white
    warmed as it was
        when he first wore it

before the fever
    burned through him
        and shrank him away

and his shipmates
    dressed him in it
        for burial – left him

in perfect cold
    intact and like himself
        then strayed in twos and

threes or however
    they lay here and there
        obscurely in their clothing

FLÂNEUR

The street's a thing of nature
    till I saunter out   it overlays itself
            continuously   sheen on a puddle
stirs   and is sombre again   the church
    has been converted
                    but I
      speed it all up   jiggle the wind
round the board outside the café   calligraphed
    in three colours of chalk   at last
      it topples   she   the café woman
and her patient husband who loves her   argue
    avoidably   yet a child's glove
      worn for days by a spear of railing
that's still damp
          it's not
    that child who's called to   darling
      put on your coat and we'll be off
(past the *flâneur*)   it's another   a child talking
    of unicorns   they're not like horses
      they're white   always   aren't they
they're mythical beasts   so an artist
    could paint one but not see it

FOR

For the night window to slant
above my bed.

For my dimensions to be what they are
with the cleanliness of a fossil

in rock, that is distinct
but is nevertheless and also rock.

For a foothold in air, the far
side of the glass, to admire how I lie.

FOR EXAMPLE

Let me explain. What we call *one another*
is a disturbance in ourselves, settled

in the world. Take a poem of my own
in the voice of somebody we might say

being careless, thinks he's Jesus. It's a man
though I'm a woman. He could be mad

but he's himself and knows it. And then
not invented, real this time, a man

next to the wall in a packed, half-lit room
who fans himself with his hat. Shadow

opens and shuts neatly behind him,
like a butterfly with one wing but entire –

he was a black man and close in tone
to his shadow in that room with no edges.

My first man (white? mad?) sees his own
disturbance match as it must, in part

at least, Jesus'. He has been born, will die
and why not rise again as if he were

a shadow on a wall who'd keep time
as the Saviour fanned himself with his hat.

The 'poem of my own' is *When I came back*

17

FOR SHAUN GREENHALGH

This one's for you, Shaun, though you
prefer to make your own and didn't ask.

If I could have something of yours I'd
like an Amarna princess, but for what,

to idle among my sad things losing all
her beauty and truth. Make me a skull,

a Damien Hirst. Wouldn't a fake or two
restore it, put back the wink and grin,

the ease it had with art and cash until
it went out in the world? Think it over –

you can do that in prison. Once you're
home in Bolton busy in your shed, we'll

bequeath you skulls, nothing less than
original and faithful under its diamonds.

I, HEN

'I am the one/Who sounds loudest in my head'
Edwin Brock *The Song of the Battery Hen*

O the racket of me
the cacophony
the choir
of auburn-feathered

yellow-beaked
tenants in
my fluorescent
white-walled head

O my open beak
my beak
open yellow
my yellow beak open

sounding the 'I'
I am –
the 'I' sounding
its loudest loudness

O the loud-headed-
and-beaked
choir of
me – auburn hen-me

sounding my loud
at these soft
mirrors of
me – I sound of them

I MIGHT

I might
    with a blow to the head
come to believe
    what's good for me, feel
what I ought, be
    the widow for example
of a soldier.
    I'd raise a girl who
can't grasp
    'never' and a boy
he never saw
    though I'm ambivalent
at best about armed
    conflict and its outcomes
both the vengeful
    and the mawkish. To be
ringed with smiles
    here in a print dress,
against the odds
    duly recovered from my
blow to the head,
    is insufficient comfort.

IN MEMORIAM

The air he died in travels round the building
now he's been taken out. Before, it kept
close to him at his door on the third landing

curled like a dog. On duty. Reprimanding
askers of questions till perhaps it slept
and let us in. It travels round the building –

ghost of a dog, malodorous and demanding
where I've flung windows open to eject
its master. At the door on the third landing

as I go past, I want bouquets and candling
to coax it home. It's not where I expect,
the air he died in. Travels round the building

until it's me that follows the bewildering
stench, more vegetable in it than flesh,
pausing to take it in. Frankly, the landing

will settle soon and the odour of his ending
revert to absence like a waived debt.
Yet air he died in's all over the building,
him in its arms, borne from the third landing.

JOE PASSED AWAY

He was a regular. Every time
he'd pick up his manners

where he left them, and a smile
that allows, yes, rules were broken,

half withheld. He'd make a pound
each from he knew who.

It's not instantaneous, passing away.
You're eased off the streets

drunk on anything you can get,
into a no-man's-land of kindliness

with half a mind you'd think
to turn you back, but no, it's heaven

for you, the bastards all in white.
Your mother's there. You ask

her as you did strangers on earth
why if she loved you she gave you birth.

JOSTLE

Then he does this:
touches you with a small, available object
like a pencil
 (*).
 You can't see anything
in the helmet he's devised except (projected
a pace or two ahead) your own back
and a point
 (*)
 of contact at your shoulder-blade
that opens into a caress. The subject (you
and all of them)
is aware of a step forward
almost taken
into the other (favoured) self.

 As if you'd catch yourself up
on the experimenter's screen
in that body
 (*)
 (yours)
or in old footage on TV
among the marchers, having run off
after all against the bomb and its obediences.
The girl at home watching, missing the rub
of shoulders − she's
erased herself and here she is
in the jostle
 (*)
 where you can't help but follow.

OCTOBER

In the mist the tower block
is without substance

and the hill beyond it, lost,
where he'll go to work

in his trilby and a pale
belted mac, flipping pages

in his notepad as he writes up
the resplendences of trees.

He has to watch his step
on damp pavements

but he sees a leaf
so uncoloured, so pearly

he looks up at last and there's
the sky, an unhinged blue.

His task is, as always,
to report back on the present

and on previous reds and golds.
The trees assert their shape

against the sky and each other
with a fierceness unseen

in green summer. It adds up
to one more October

that, in his newly rent heart,
he doubts his powers to tell of.

ORPHEUS

When he gets out of jail
        he won't
                go palely
                        loitering, he'll go
                straight to town, make her
see sense. Her name's Irene –
        in Greek
                it means "peace".

But she'll say no.

Did she see him dither –
        not sure in the smoke,
                the din, the toss of frills
& feathers
        & flawless
                high kicks,
        which garter was hers?

Poets, she'll snap. Look round.
        Look round I tell you,
                I can have my pick – if
a poet was what I wanted.
        She'll jerk a thumb.
                It's that way
        to the river.
                        Go & cool off.

        He will.
Goodnight. Goodnight.
        His head will sing.

SHOPPING WITH GARBO

Garbo was older like a sister
who'd done everything first

so as the younger girl put on
lipstick the calligraphy of too

many too lovely photographs
was everywhere, all she'd do

was apply it. Latterly, as one
they forswore beauty, taking

to mackintosh and headscarf
worn in silence but it was her

now, the wiser. She'd defend
them both with a single ivory

knight, solemn and avuncular,
who'd move obliquely against

danger and who sidestepped
into her pocket, out shopping.

TO BE A GHOST

To be a ghost
    is to unwind
        into light – no

to be unwound
    or – anyhow
        you're run up

against this,
    the rotating O –
        of course, that is

how it ended
    but such a thin
        ribbon of frames,

dubbed or
    what? Lack of a
        footfall tells you

you're dead –
    can't shake that
        out of your ears –

yet you stalk,
    stalk and mutter.
        To haunt is to be

bound – not
    to the living
        in their obscurity

but a machine
    all wheels for
        ticking you away

on the blank-
      faced and o-so-
            easy-virtue screen –

no chance
      you'd trust them
            if you could help it.

TURNER'S HOUSE

Light strips the trees
    and ghosts the windows

till they pass
    through one another freely

and the square rooms
    frame and reframe themselves

for whoever there is.
    "I am here," says Light.

"I have stepped into your shoes
    for the sake of the more suggestible

caller. Dust motes and I
    obscure for them your prolonged absence.

They do not overhear
    my remarks and if they did,

no matter. They would smile
    and enquire to whom I am speaking."

UNMAPPING THE GLOBE

Begin with words.

Stare hard enough and they'll
lift off, letting go
their blackness. The lettered
surface will expand until, looking
over your shoulder, you'll see
mirror places,
huge, illegible, gone.

Unbrush the varnish.

Everywhere glue thins
to liquid. Ocean's moist again
as it was before the fresh work dried,
and continents too
have loosened. Peel back
the twelve daisy-petals of paper
each three lines of longitude in width.
Dark coastline trailing islands
into marble-painted sea
will separate where it was matched
edge to edge. Land mass
threaded with rivers will curl away
in navigators' segments.

Loves me. Loves me not.

Take the blank sphere
out of its housing. It can't spin
and doesn't know what waiting
is, inert and dreamless
till the new map-makers arrive.

WAIL

Consider the child on the bus,
not seen but wailing.

I speak, and with assurance,
for all of us. We shrink

inside our large coats
except the mother whose child

keeps her warm. Today is cold.
If hot we'd swell

as one. Like us, she'd work
at unsticking skin off skin.

Wail, child, while you can.
It is permitted to the innocent

whose wail has no subtext.
Wail for us. Not for our several

griefs, but on our behalf.
We are where you are, the place

of wailing. In this place
we were not ever, cannot ever

be bathed, powdered or fed.
Hell is that small. That incidental.

WHAT COLOUR IS THE SEA?

Every evening a dog barks
in the stairwell.
Separate from our talk –

though that too echoes
off tiled walls –
the bark's inflection's not

unlike human complaint
as if the dog
hoped earlier for better.

*

Out by the car-hire, a child
sat and wept,
nobody to address

with her sorrow. Them,
gone so long?
All she could do with grit

was done already, trickled
in low heaps
like sand, to each a fistful.

*

Making arcs with his arm
over the table-top
a waiter mopped coffee

spilt from the upset cup
of a blind man
in dark glasses and a bold

holiday shirt. His wife,
was it, dabbed
his front for dark splashes.

*

The sea continues green
blue, gold, silver,
lilac – odd to put names

to colours picked up idly
and returned
all as one, with its own

authority, or a din not far
off absolute
but overridden by gulls.

WHEN I CAME BACK

When I came back it was all changed
even my date of birth. It has

to do with prophecy, so I understand
but don't ask how it happened,

came about, was made to be, contrary
to what we know of time as lived

and history as record. Or memory
as remembered. I'll become troubled

then, asking aloud whether my date of
death can shift, and other people's,

to before our own births, gone in one single
overwhelming re-adjustment. Or put off

with no false account of the causes and effects
of resurrection, but our undoings undone.